The Emperor's Egg

There are **seventeen** kinds of penguin,
but the Emperor is the only one that breeds in
Antarctica in midwinter. The adults arrive at their
breeding areas — often more than 100 miles from
the open sea — in late autumn. A few weeks later
the female lays her single egg and returns to the
sea, leaving the male to keep the egg warm until
it hatches a couple of months later.

At first the male and female take turns caring
for the chick. But soon it is big enough
to be left while both parents go fishing for
its food in the sea. By the time it is
four months old, the young penguin's coat
of down has been replaced by adult feathers.
It now also sets off for the sea,
where it has to start taking care of itself.

For James, John, Steve, Tim and Tony —
and all the other dads
M. J.

For Mum and Dad,
from egg number one!
J. C.

ISBN 0-439-18806-7

Text copyright © 1999 by Martin Jenkins.
Illustrations copyright © 1999 by Jane Chapman.
All rights reserved. Published by Scholastic Inc.,
555 Broadway, New York, NY 10012,
by arrangement with Candlewick Press.
SCHOLASTIC and associated logos are trademarks
and/or registered trademarks of Scholastic Inc.

12 11 10 9   3 4 5 6/0

Printed in the U.S.A.   40

First Scholastic printing, January 2001

This book was typeset in Humana.
The illustrations were done in acrylics.

The Emperor's Egg

Martin Jenkins

illustrated by Jane Chapman

SCHOLASTIC INC.

New York Toronto London Auckland Sydney
Mexico City New Delhi Hong Kong

Down at the very bottom of the world, there's a huge island that's almost completely covered in snow and ice. It's called Antarctica, and it's the coldest, windiest place on Earth.

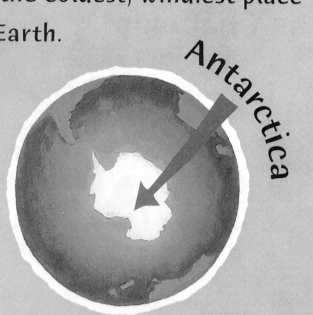

Antarctica

The weather's bad enough there in summer, but in winter it's really terrible.

It's hard to imagine anything actually living there.

But wait...
what's that shape over there?
It can't be.

Yes!

It's a penguin!

It's not just any old penguin either.
It's a male Emperor penguin
(the biggest penguin in the world),
and he's doing a Very Important Job.

He's taking care of his egg.

Male Emperor penguins are about 4 feet tall.

The females are a little smaller.

He didn't lay it himself, of course.

His mate did that
a few weeks ago.

But very soon
afterward
she turned around
and waddled off
to the sea.

That's where female Emperor penguins
spend most of the winter — swimming about,
getting as fat as they can
eating as much as they can,
and generally having a very nice time
(as far as you can tell)!

Emperor penguins eat mainly fish, squid, and tiny shrimplike animals called krill.

Which leaves
the father penguin
stuck on the ice with
his egg.

Now, the most important
thing about egg-sitting is
to stop your egg from
getting cold.

Inside the egg, a penguin chick is starting to grow.

If the egg gets cold, the chick will die.

That means it has
to be kept off the ice
and out of the wind.

And what better
way to do that than
to rest it on your feet
and tuck it right up
under your tummy?

Which is just what the father penguin does.

13

And that's how he'll stay for two whole months,
until his egg is ready to hatch.

Can you imagine it?
Standing around in the freezing cold
with an egg on your feet
for **two whole** months?

Female Emperor penguins lay one egg in May or June,
which is the beginning of winter in Antarctica.

What's more, there's nothing for the father penguin to eat on land.

So that means two whole months with an egg on your feet **and no dinner!**

I don't know about you

And because he's egg-sitting,
he can't go off to the sea to feed.

Or breakfast

or lunch

or snacks.

but I'd be **very, very** miserable.

Luckily, the penguins don't seem to mind
too much. They have thick feathers and lots of
fat under their skin to help keep them warm.

And when it gets really cold and
windy, they all snuggle up together
and shuffle over the ice in a great big huddle

Most of the time, the huddle trundles along
very, very slowly.

But **sometimes,**

when the penguins get to a particularly slippery slope...

they slide down it on their tummies,
pushing themselves along
with their flippers,
always remembering
to take care of their egg —
and trying hard not to bump into each other.

Even though the males keep the egg tucked up tight under their tummies when they slide, it sometimes rolls out and breaks.

And that's how the father penguin
spends the winter.

Until one day he hears a chip, chip, chip.

His egg is starting to hatch.
It takes a day or so, but finally the egg
cracks right open —

and out pops a penguin chick.

Now the father penguin
has two jobs to do.
He has to keep
the chick warm

and he has to feed it.

*The chick is only about 6 inches tall at first,
and much too small to keep warm by itself.*

But on what? The chick is too small to be taken off to the sea to catch food, and it can't be left behind on the ice.

Well, deep down in the father penguin's throat, there's a pouch where he makes something a little like milk. And that's what he feeds to his hungry chick.

The father penguin can make only enough of the
milky stuff to feed his chick for a couple of weeks.
But just as he's about to run out,
a dot appears on the horizon.

It gets closer
and closer
and yes!

It's mom!

She starts trumpeting "hello"
and the father penguin
starts trumpeting "hello"
and the chick whistles.

The racket goes on for hours,
and it really does sound as if they're
extremely pleased to see each other.

Every adult penguin has its own special call, like a fingerprint.

Chicks have their own special whistle, too.

As soon as things have calmed down,
the mother penguin is sick — right
into her chick's mouth!

Yuk,

you may think.

Yum,

thinks the chick,

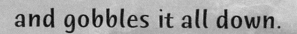

and gobbles it all down.

It's the mother's turn to take care of
the chick now, while the father sets off
to the sea for a well-earned meal of his own.

About time, too!

INDEX

Antarctica......3, 6, 15

chick......3, 12, 22–29

egg......3, 8, 12–15, 20–22

feathers......3, 18

female penguin......3, 8, 10–11, 15, 26–29

food......3, 11, 16–17, 23–25, 28–29

hatching......3, 22

huddling......18–19

keeping warm......3, 12–13, 18–19, 23

male penguin......3, 8, 12–26, 29

sea......3, 10–11, 24, 29

size......8, 23

sliding......20–21

trumpeting......26–27

whistling......26–27

Look up the pages to find out about all these penguin things.
Don't forget to look at both kinds of word — **this kind** *and* **this kind.**